BANNERS EXHIBITION

*... a millennium project by
the Church of Scotland Guild*

Edited by
Elma Stuart and Fiona Lange

THE CHURCH OF SCOTLAND GUILD

SAINT ANDREW PRESS
Edinburgh

First published in 2001 by
Saint Andrew Press
121 George Street, Edinburgh EH2 4YN

on behalf of
The Church of Scotland Guild
121 George Street
Edinburgh EH2 4YN
0131 225 5722
Direct Line   0131 240 2217
e-mail   *guild@cofscotland.org.uk*
www.cos-guild.org.uk

Scripture quotation taken from the Holy Bible, New International Version. Copyright
© 1973, 1978, 1984 by International Bible Society. First published in Great Britain
1979. Used by permission of Hodder & Stoughton Ltd, a member of the Hodder
Headline Group. All rights reserved. 'NIV' is a trademark of International Bible Society.
UK trademark number 1448790.

ISBN 0 86153 323 2

British Library Cataloguing in Publication Data
A catalogue record for this book is available from the British Library

Manufactured in Great Britain by The Bath Press

CONTENTS

INTRODUCTION

'Whose we are and Whom we serve'

The Church of Scotland Guild has a long history of taking ideas and turning them into reality. Founded in 1887 as a vehicle for women to harness their talents in the work of the church, it was the sole medium for women to use their skills in the practical expression of their faith.

The largest voluntary organisation in Scotland primarily for women, the Guild is no longer the only channel for women in the wider work of the church. However, in today's congregations, you will find that if anything needs done, often the best thing to do is ask the Guild!

It is from this background that the Guild millennium project, the banner exhibition, *Hold out the Word of Life*, grew and took shape.

The Banner Exhibition came to epitomise and encapsulate the aim of this empowering movement:

> *to invite and encourage members to commit their lives to Jesus Christ and enabled them to express their faith in worship, prayer and action*

WORSHIP The banners are a reflection of the Word of God – the books of the Bible in picture form.

PRAYER The exhibition arose from prayer; was enabled, supported and carried through by the prayers of guildmembers across the country.

ACTION The exhibition could not have taken place without the action of 44,000 guildmembers, their friends and relatives from many denominations, joining together to create and produce the banners and stands.

As Convener and Secretary of the Banners 2000 Committee, we feel deeply honoured and privileged, if that is not too clichéd, to have been involved in the staging of this exhibition. At various moments, and even occasionally all at the same time, it has been a source of stress and yet a joy in the heart; exhausting and yet exhilarating; the stuff of nightmares but mostly of dreams come true.

For all of you who saw the banners on their tour or who took part in the exhibition – but perhaps particularly for those of you who did not see the beautiful banners – we very much hope you enjoy this book and the brief glimpse into our memories!

ELMA STUART, *Convener*

FIONA LANGE, *Secretary*

Church of Scotland Guild

Banners 2000 Committee

April 2001

SECTION ONE

Committee Comments

The Banners 2000 Committee consists of the following members:

ELMA STUART, *Convener*
(Elgin)

MARGARET WOTHERSPOON
(Castle Douglas)

MYRA GOSKIRK
(Lairg)

MYRA FISHER
(Glasgow)

LIZ STURROCK
(Dundee)

MARGARET CASHMAN
(Galashiels)

MAGGIE LUNAN
(Glasgow)

CATHERINE NELSON
(Stonehouse)

FIONA LANGE, *Secretary*
(Guild Information Officer, Edinburgh)

Following the completion of the planning stage of the exhibition, the big day rolled round – 10 January 2000. The exhibition opened in Wellington Church, Glasgow. The committee was to set up the banners at the beginning and dismantle them at the end to familiarise themselves with the idiosyncrasies of each of the banners. A committee member helped at each of the venues – to co-ordinate and support the organising groups in each area. Here are their views at the culmination of an eventful year:

ELMA STUART (CONVENER)

It was in 1995 when Mary Sherrard, then Guild National President, asked guild members to think of a millennium project. I was asked if I would take this forward. I became immersed in it; so much so, that when friends saw me approaching, their thoughts were, 'How can we get her off the subject of Banners 2000?'!

It was a project with so much potential, but what would be the theme?

The members of the small committee were puzzled, to say the least! We had a break of two weeks to consider and report back with brilliant ideas – and no excuses!

A problem shared is a problem solved … and so my husband asked 'How many guild councils did you say there were?' I replied, 'sixty-six'. 'Well, don't you know that there are sixty-six Books in the Bible?' was his reply.

Next meeting, a few suggestions – no particular enthusiasm. I then related my 'discovery' and the idea was born. God does indeed move in mysterious ways!

Early in 1996, each guild presbyterial council was allocated a book of the Bible. Notes on banner-making were given to every guild. Puzzlement, fear, lack of skill, but mostly enthusiasm, ran wild in the guilds. The banner committee members travelled around to encourage – and Carberry Tower offered courses. 'Banners 2000' was on its way!

What about a National Banner? This would provide a centrepiece and focus for the whole event.

It would not be easy – it would involve much discussion, and banner-making skills. Maggie and I, with the assistance of keen banner-makers – Ina Calder, Grangemouth; Daphne Colvin-Smith, Selkirk; Mary Hunter, Aberdeen; Jean Low, Glasgow; Anne Mahoney, West Lothian; Marjory MacFarlane, Perthshire; and Yvonne Pearson, Moray – became the team which would create the National Banner

Thoughts were tossed about for several meetings. It was finally agreed that the banner must speak for itself to young and old alike, especially those outside the church, with an up-to-date message. One member woke one morning with the image of the World Wide Web, and we were on our way! Other 'Webs' – webs of deceit, lies, money, debt, loneliness, worthlessness – have so many people in their grip.

The group shared the overwhelming sense that they longed for everyone to know that they are loved, that to be born is to be chosen – and that this truth will set us all free. It all came together in the National Banner! (See picture number 67.) It was a particular thrill when the National Banner was displayed during the General Assembly, in May 2000.

So what could we do with sixty-seven banners, once they were completed? A display at the Guild Annual Meeting? Yes, but what then? A march from 121 to the Assembly Hall? No, the banners would have to be specially made with holes to allow the wind to pass through; that would not be practical! So, back to the Annual Meeting display, with one banner from each Council plus our National Banner. At our next meeting, a request came for banners to be displayed in Cathedral Cities. Then, 'What about Whithorn?' 'That's a long way.' Then, 'What about Orkney?' 'That's even farther!'

And so it evolved.

On 10 January 2000, the exhibition opened in Wellington Church, Glasgow. It has since travelled the length and breadth of Scotland, even to Whithorn and to Orkney, from Oban to Aberdeen! A day to set up the exhibition – a day to dismantle and transport – a day to set up and open again in the next location in over twenty locations all over Scotland – and then, to London in 2001!

None of this would have been possible without the dedicated help of so many people: Fiona Lange, the Guild Information Officer; handymen; church members and friends; ministers. They all did far more than could ever have been expected and their efforts have been much appreciated.

I would like to conclude with some of the many comments from schoolchildren who saw the exhibition:

> 'At first I thought it would be boring, but in fact it was fun and the time flew past.'

> 'I would encourage everyone to go, even if they don't normally go to church. Perhaps they might go back.'

> 'Classy as owt!' – which I think means she liked it a lot, as so many of all ages did!

ES

FIONA LANGE (SECRETARY TO THE COMMITTEE)

Very much the 'Johnny come lately' of the committee, I joined the Guild as Information Officer in December 1998. Soon after that, Alison Twaddle, General Secretary, asked if I'd heard of the banners that were being created across the country. Did I fancy organising a lorry to take them to a few venues? As the 'keen newcomer', what else could I say: 'Of course – no problem!'

It seems that I get the blame for suggesting that it would be easier to keep the banners on the move than find storage areas for them. That, it seems, encouraged Elma to whisper in even more people's ears, and encourage many more churches to throw open their doors to what was, after all, an unknown quantity – real faith in the future!

The big thrust for me came in December 1999, bringing the banners together, organising publicity material, information and advice packs for the organising groups in each area, and ensuring that everyone from the van company to the person with the church keys knew when the banners were coming.

When someone asked me how I felt about the banners after having worked with them for so long and having organised the logistics of the year-long exhibition, I replied that I loved them like my own children. She responded that she knew what an up-and-down relationship that could be!

Everyone who has been a part of this exhibition, whether on committee, at local level, or as a visitor, has been truly overwhelmed by the impact of such a body of beautiful, inspirational work.

I had lived with pictures and photographs of the banners since long before the exhibition started in January 2000. Dare I say it, I was even a bit blasé about them – they were all great, all colourful, all fabulous, let's just get them on the move! I was more concerned that they arrived where and when they were supposed to! Nothing, however, prepared me for the impact they had as a composite. At the first location, Wellington Church in Glasgow, members of the committee themselves would be responsible for the setting up and dismantling to ensure they understood the implications for future venues. All was going well, if not very quickly! At the end of a long day, Elma Stuart and I were satisfied that the banners were all up and were tidying away a few bits and pieces. Both at once we looked up from what we were doing (actually we were capering and she hit me with a screwdriver – such is the way of the Guild!), and, as if for the first time, saw the banners as one vision ... and we both gasped. It was an incredibly moving moment and one which, without fail, was repeated at every location. Each venue added a certain quality to the banners, different lighting seemed to highlight a different banner, shift the emphasis and send a different message on each occasion! No surprise then that it was not uncommon to hear of people visiting for a second or even third time, and bringing with them friends and neighbours, keen that no-one they knew should miss the opportunity to be touched by these banners.

On a personal note, the banner exhibition has been a wonderful thing to be part of. To join in with such an inspirational effort, to be part of such a significant event, can be life-changing and life-enhancing, as can the truly good friends you make along the way.

Thank you, Elma.

FJL

LIZ STURROCK

Sitting on a train with Elma Stuart, quite a number of years ago, I was asked if I would like to be on a banner committee. My first thought was: 'I know nothing about banners', but, nevertheless, I ended up on the committee. After many meetings, I began to realise what was involved! It was frightening when the year 2000 arrived and we were ready to launch the banner exhibition in Glasgow; I had no idea what I was in for! After struggling with stands, banners and yet more stands, and yet more banners, we got the exhibition set up and ready. Hours of hard work and not a little confusion had paid off. Here they were – the books of the Bible in splendid glory – created by the skills and talents of guildmembers everywhere, for all to see.

LS

MYRA GOSKIRK

It has been difficult to pin-point my own personal highlights of the exhibition, as everything was so special!

The Dornoch exhibition was particularly memorable for me, with its vast numbers, including many bus tours and visitors just stopping to view the cathedral and finding the added bonus of the exhibition! They were delighted to be there and they often requested information on future dates and venues so that they could see them again!

The welcome I received in Orkney, from everyone I met while there, how they had 'grabbed the opportunity' to have the banners on home ground, was another highlight. The commitment of everyone on Orkney was marvellous to behold – the congregation used the banners as a basis for a whole summer of worship!

On a more personal note, a vivid memory is of setting up the banners at the Annual Meeting in the Royal Concert Hall in Glasgow. There, my husband and I worked alongside a lady from Renfield St Stephens, Glasgow. We blethered away while working and after some time we realised that we had been friends as teenagers and this friendship was quickly recalled and renewed. What a lot of catching up was done that day – very much an unexpected bonus, all thanks to the banners!

It has been a privilege and a great blessing to serve on the committee for the past few years and the Lord has patiently led us, not only to flourish-ing friendships with each other but also to a greater understanding of His Will, with this venture to 'Hold out the Word of Life' throughout 2000 and beyond.

MG

Margaret Cashman

It is strange that my memories of the banner exhibition should predominately be of people – and of how God works through people. The banners were magnificent. Each one portrayed in its own individual way an interpretation of one book of the Bible – perhaps through illustrating a verse, or perhaps the theme of the book or one striking story from its content. The beauty and skilled workmanship of the banners spoke to me of the many, many people who had worked together under the guidance of God to produce each work of art.

There are the memories of the people who helped set up the exhibition in each venue – many of them not guildmembers but volunteers from the congregations involved. They put in hours of work, getting more and more excited as the exhibition took shape, and the sheer beauty of it spurred them on to greater effort.

Then there was that dreadful moment in one venue when every package had been counted in – but the National Banner was missing! Only a piece or two of the stand could be found! Headlines from the Guild Newsletter flashed before my eyes 'National Banner lost in transit'! I felt that would have been the end of any connection I might have with the Guild! No-one who had been party to losing the National Banner could hold up their head again! Imagine my relief when, an hour or two later, the National Banner was discovered rolled up within another one – all the helpers rejoiced! We felt like characters in the Biblical story of the woman who lost her coin and rejoiced when she found it.

I remember the people I met through the Banner Exhibition as individuals, and I also remember the pleasure we had in working together. I could name many individuals but refrain from doing so, as none deserves credit more than another. However, the names of two people keep recurring as I reflect on the banners – two people who made a remarkable contribution to the whole concept of the exhibition and its implementation. I refer to Elma and John Stuart. I was present at the National Executive when Elma raised the idea of banners and the Millennium, and the go-ahead was given for further discussion. From then on, Elma's quiet, determined leadership, her ability to motivate others and her sheer hard work, inspired us all to produce and stage an exhibition which brought glory to God and inspired many to look at their Bible again. Their spirit and commitment sum up for me the spirit and commitment of people all over the country who worked so hard under God to stage this memorable exhibition. As the old hymn puts it: 'To God be the glory, great things He hath done.'

MC

MYRA FISHER

In the James Stewart film, *The Glenn Miller Story*, his wife tells him she has a prickly sensation on the back of her neck when something extraordinary is happening. It was exactly that feeling that I had when I stood on the chancel at Wellington Church and looked at a sanctuary decorated with the banners. A thrill of excitement came over me! I was tired and hungry and was longing for a shower, but that feeling of wonder at what the committee had undertaken will always be with me.

Staging the exhibition at the Royal Concert Hall was wonderful; as it was, also, at the cathedral and museum in Glasgow. I have vivid memories of all the tourists who came to see the beautiful buildings as well as the beautiful banners! One lady from Dublin was particularly enthusiastic and I found her photographing the Dunfermline banner as a memento. It transpired that she had been baptized in Dunfermline!

Another highlight of a leg of the tour on which I helped was at Hamilton: the dedication service for the banners was wonderful.

I have often wondered why I was asked to join the committee, but I have enjoyed the work, the fellowship and friendship of all the others so much, I thank God I was!

MF

MARGARET WOTHERSPOON

It WAS and still IS a great surprise to me to find myself a member of the banner committee; what started out as a committee of guildmembers has grown into a group of friends who have shared so many experiences over the years.

Working on the committee and sharing in the setting up of some of the stages of the tour has been a bit of an adventure! I can still feel the pangs of nerves as I set out to meet the team at my first venue. 'O ye of little faith' springs to mind, as I discovered they were well organised, bubbling with enthusiasm, and could not have been more welcoming!

Two unforgettable impressions come to mind. Firstly, the dedication of a guildmember who had come straight from night duty in a hospital to be one of the team to set up the exhibtion. This level of dedication was repeated in so many ways. Secondly, the picture of no fewer than two ministers watching one of their wives having great difficulty in fitting a banner into its tubular holder while they held the tube steady with their feet! These ministers, what are they like!

MW

CATHERINE NELSON

The banner exhibition has been, for me, a most exciting project. It was thrilling in the early days, watching the first seeds of the idea being sown … and the excitement mounted. The idea caught on at training days and banner workshops from the Borders to the Outer Hebrides; and, during my year as National Convener, I had the privilege of seeing many of them being made and was there at various rallies when Councils selected the one which would represent them on the tour; finally, the whole idea coming to fruition at exhibitions up and down the country.

This is the Guild at its best – united action!

Every guildmember, from Shetland to London, has played their part in 'Holding out the Word of Life' in a new way to thousands of people!

CN

MAGGIE LUNAN

When I came to write this piece, I realised that, for me, Elma _is_ Banners 2000; she is a banner for the Guild – all that it should represent – a living message of a loving God to all who meet her.

Looking back to the first meetings, I remember Elma's enthusiasm and optimism – her assurance that it would work. Throughout the whole process of preparation she elicited different people's gifts and affirmed their contributions. She served the committee, listened to their doubts and worries and kept pointing us all in the right direction. In the making of the banner, as we struggled to hear God's Word and not be waylaid by people's expectations, she was a solid rock – 'this is what it is about' … 'of course it takes time' … it's Elma's laughter, her willingness for any task … and always that extra touch – the encouraging phone call, the thank-you note, the tin of home baking!

And then the tour – never did we imagine it would be such an undertaking – carrying boxes, checking off lists, hunting the scissors or the tape! Elma and her husband, John, were often at the thick of it – their commitment acted as example and encouragement.

Elma's faith and joy and commitment IS the message.

ML

SECTION TWO

VENUES

The Banner Exhibition was staged at each of the following venues:

Wellington Church, **Glasgow**	from 11 January 2000
St Michael's Church, **Linlithgow**	from 2 February 2000
St Giles Church, **Elgin**	from 2 March 2000
St Rufus Church, **Keith**	from 21 March 2000
The Caird Hall, **Dundee**	from 3 April 2000
The Old Church, **Kelso**	from 11 April 2000
St Machar's Cathedral, **Aberdeen**	from 6 May 2000
Old High Church, **Inverness**	from 27 May 2000
Dornoch Cathedral, **Dornoch**	from 9 June 2000
Kirkwall East Church, **Orkney**	from 26 June 2000
Kilmore & Oban Church, **Oban**	from 5 July 2000
St Columba's Church, **Ayr**	from 1 August 2000
St Ninian's Priory, **Whithorn**	from 9 August 2000
Royal Concert Hall, **Glasgow**	Guild Annual Meeting 26 August 2000
St Mungo Museum, **Glasgow** Glasgow Cathedral	from 28 August 2000
St Matthew's Church, **Perth**	from 5 September 2000
Greyfriars Church, **Dumfries**	from 26 September 2000
St John's Church, **Hamilton**	from 10 October 2000
St Andrew's & St George's Church, **Edinburgh**	from 31 October 2000
Kirkcaldy Museum, **Kirkcaldy**	from 8 December 2000
St Columba's Church, **London**	from 11 January 2001

SECTION THREE

This section gives a brief description of the banner submitted by each Guild Presbyterial Council, and what it represents. In some instances, those who have created the banner have given further details and stories of their involvement with the Banner Exhibition.

1

EDINBURGH NORTH

GENESIS

In the beginning God created ...

In six days, sea and land; day and night; fish and animals; man and woman

When the Lord saw how wicked everyone in the world was ...

He sent a flood and Noah built an ark

The famine was so severe, the people of Egypt and Canaan became weak with hunger ...

Joseph, an interpreter of dreams, became Governor of Egypt and through his actions the people were saved from starvation.

It was definitely a learning experience from the first of many readings of the book – through to the choice of materials. Every time we saw the banners all together at any of the exhibition venues, we saw something different!

The image on the quilt reads: IN THE BEGINNING GOD CREATED

2

EDINBURGH EAST

EXODUS

Moses on Mount Sinai

In the book of Exodus, the Lord gives Moses the Ten Commandments, which we strive to live by today.

When we thought of Exodus, we thought about Moses and that he should be the central figure and that, although there were so many major events to choose from, the most important was the Ten Commandments. We computer-generated Moses' face on to fabric, as no one in our group was very artistic!

We did enjoy making the banner and the pooling of ideas. We got the Hebrew for the Commandments from the Internet and the material for Moses' tunic was collected from the wool rubbed off by sheep on to wire fences, hand-woven and dyed with natural colours. So we used very old methods and very new technology. None in our group are expert seamstresses, artists or great ideas people but together it is amazing what we can achieve.

3

WEST LOTHIAN

LEVITICUS

Ye may eat of their fruit

The Book of Leviticus was so named because it concerns the laws relating to the Hebrew religion; oversight of which was in the hands of the Levitical priesthood. These laws strengthened the spiritual life of the people. The book is generally accredited to Moses and was written around 1400 BC.

The verse was chosen for its simplicity and for its 'wide horizons'.

The design shows a tree, its white trunk and branches based on the Menorah, with the fruits of the earth growing on the blue and gold, which represents the world. Around the earth, triangles of colour represent a rainbow and this reminds us of God's covenant.

Mention of the fruits can be found in both the Old and New Testaments; the pomegranate, the fig, the olive and the vine.

YE MAY EAT OF THEIR FRUIT.
LEVITICUS   CH 19   V25

4

EDINBURGH SOUTH

NUMBERS

I am the Lord Your God

Exploring the book of Numbers seemed, at first, a daunting task. However, after a lot of reading and prayer, we found that there was a lot within this book for the Council banner! We chose this verse because God provided for, as well as punished, the people of Israel.

Once the verse was chosen, the fun began! What design do we use; what materials; everyone had their own ideas and suggestions! However, some of us had seen the stained glass window in St Andrew's and St George's Church, Edinburgh, and the pictorial window with the open Bible at its head inspired us. Then we decided which stories to use from Numbers.

All were agreed that the fun and fellowship from this is still with us, and although we had different skills, we all contributed in some way!

5

GLASGOW NORTH

DEUTERONOMY

The Lord Himself will lead you and be with you

Taken from chapter 31, verse 8, we thought this was a very suitable text to lead us into the new Millennium.

6

LOTHIAN EAST

JOSHUA

We will serve the Lord

The banner depicts Joshua and family outside the walls of Jericho, with the River Jordan and stones alongside.

This was chosen as it has a positive message. Joshua and family could represent any family.

When we first heard of the request to make banners, we said 'Let's do it!' Not that we are experts, far from it, but we had made banners a few years before. This time we had a great laugh; drawing sketches and plans, choosing the right colour of material, deciding who would do what and then using a computer for the letters!

7

Lothian West

Judges

God is our strength

31

8

MELROSE

RUTH

Your way shall be my way

This text was chosen, from chapter 1, verse 16, because we felt it truly represents the Book of Ruth. It depicts Ruth and her mother-in-law walking along a winding road, which is lined with corn and has, in the background, hills which are a representation of the three Eildon Hills which dominate the central Borders.

The Guild group, whose banner was chosen, is fortunate to have a member who is an artist. She drew up several sketches and all the members chose the final design. A group of six volunteers, led by the artist, then met on a weekly basis for about six months to make the banner. A bring-and-buy sale was held to raise the money required for material.

YOUR WAY shall be MY WAY
YOUR GOD MY GOD

RUTH

A.D. 2000   St. Boswells Guild

9

IRVINE & KILMARNOCK

1ST SAMUEL

Here I am

This passage from Samuel, chapter 3, verses 4–9, was chosen because we felt it depicted the Guild motto, 'Whose we are and Whom we serve'. It was also felt that at the beginning of a new Millennium there was a need for re-commitment and a sense of looking forward to the next 1,000 years.

A large-scale drawing was produced, with the help of a friend who could draw faces very well and could assist with the painting. A decision then had to be made on which symbols were to be incorporated and it was agreed to use the Ark of the Covenant, the Lamp and the Millennium Cross. When it came to the colour scheme we thought that, as this was a traditional interpretation of the story, the striking use of colour could give a 20th-century look. The selection of colours was influenced by the paintings of the Scottish colourist Arthur Melville, who worked at the end of the last century, and, in particular, one of his Mediterranean scenes was used as a basis for the banner. The lettering of the text was machine-stitched, cut out and applied to the banner.

The work was sometimes backbreaking (leaning and stretching over the frame), uncomfortable (lying on pillows underneath the banner pushing and pulling needles through the material), bruising (if the frame caught your arm) but NEVER DULL. The laughter, co-operation, commitment and expertise (not all the ladies had done much sewing) was very satisfying and uplifting.

HERE I AM

10

Peebles

2ND SAMUEL

He is my shield

A small amateur group met and were unanimous in choosing chapter 22, verses 2 and 3 as the theme for our banner, particularly emphasising the wind, shield, rock and refuge. Someone suggested a basic shape of a shield. This seemed sensible for it meant the work could be divided into five parts, which would give ease of handling and apportioning of labour.

The high tower, the cross and the sword were fairly straightforward but the rock exercised the thoughts of one member of the group for many months. WHAT does a rock look like, and how to interpret that on to fabric? During that time at every service in church, at least one hymn seemed to have reference to a rock and, while the thought of clinging to the rock was very comforting, the comfort was somewhat darkened by our inability still to visualise its physical and material representation. We looked at many photos of mountains in the Holy Land, which certainly suggested colour. We even looked at a video from a holiday in Wales, to get ideas from the mountains and even the slate quarries! It was often impossible to translate these ideas on to fabric and many attempts were discarded. Finally, an unlikely combination of material from a sari shop, encaustic art, hand-made silk paper 'lace' made on the sewing machine, using muslin and much manipulation, was decided upon and a small rock emerged!

11

ANNANDALE & ESKDALE

1ST KINGS

The verse chosen was taken from chapter 18, verse 38: 'Then the fire of the Lord fell and burned up the sacrifice, the wood, the stones and the soil, and also licked up the water in the trench.'

12

DUMFRIES

2ND KINGS

This depicts the widow's oil, taken from chapter 4, verses 1–7.

TROSTAN AND OBBLY

THE
WIDOW'S
OIL
2 KINGS

KIRKCONNEL
GUILD

13

DUNDEE

1ST CHRONICLES

This banner depicts King David in the temple.

14

GLASGOW NORTH EAST

2ND CHRONICLES

His Love is Eternal

The Jews sang when the Ark entered the temple and the verse holds true to this day and into the Millennium.

When the idea of a banner for the Millennium was introduced we were all very enthusiastic!

15

DUNS

EZRA

The Guild group which made the banner representing Duns chose the Rebuilding of the Temple, as it was felt as though they too were rebuilding their own church with their new minister.

The banner took about about two months and 200 cups of coffee to complete!

St Andrews Wallace Green
Church of Scotland Guild.

To Commemorate

The Millennium.

Ezra. The Temple Rebuilt.

In The Year Of Our Lord.

2000.

Whose we are Whom we Serve.

16

JEDBURGH EAST

NEHEMIAH

Rise and build

This was taken from chapter 2, verse 18. The first two pictures are set in building blocks; the men working from sunrise to darkness, and the guards on watch for the enemy. At the bottom are the rebuilt walls of Jerusalem. Nehemiah kneels in a prayer of thanksgiving for the work that has been done.

49

17

JEDBURGH WEST

ESTHER

The banner depicts the text from chapter 1, verses 5–7. The green and red represent the palace courtyard where King Xerxes held his banquet. Queen Vashti refused to display her beauty before his guests and so a decree, also depicted on the banner, was issued ruling that all women must honour their husbands. Vashti was also dismissed and Esther, chosen to be queen, was now in a position to save her people, the Jews.

In true Guild fashion, the creation of the banners gave us the opportunity to realise individual talents, which many of us had not had the confidence to express in the past.

When the exhibition was staged in Kelso, there was great fun and fellowship among all who helped it run so smoothly. The diversity and beauty of the banners transformed the church and we continued to notice details in them that we had not spotted before!

18

HAMILTON NORTH

JOB

Then out of the storm, the Lord spoke to Job

This banner shows scenes taken from throughout the book of Job, particularly chapters 38, 39, 40 and 41. The panels illustrate the theme 'A test of faith'.

Then out of The Storm The Lord ~ Spoke to Job

19

GLASGOW SOUTH EAST

PSALMS

Peace on Earth

This text is taken from Psalm 55, verse 6. It features a dove in flight over the earth, a symbol of peace. Peace on earth is our prayer for the Millennium.

20

KIRKCUDBRIGHT

PROVERBS

Wisdom has builded her house. She hath hewn out her seven pillars

The text is taken from chapter 9, verse 1, and seems to be the focal point for the entire book of Proverbs.

Wisdom hath builded her house

She hath hewn out her seven pillars

21

ARDROSSAN

ECCLESIASTES

Fear God and keep His Commandments

This text was chosen as it seems to summarise the whole book. We had to use home-grown products having no material shops on the island! Inspiration was close to home! The sofa upholstery looked like bark – the very thing! A spare piece of the fabric was used for the tree. A skirt remnant provided the right colour for the priest. The yellow lettering was cut from old kitchen curtains!

22

LANARK

SONG OF SOLOMON

In the Garden

A reflection on the relationship between Christ and the Church – like a lily among thorns, like an apple tree among the trees of the forest, like a young stag in the rugged hills, come south wind blow on my garden, a well of flowing water.

23

GLASGOW SOUTH WEST

ISAIAH

Here is the road. Follow it

This text is from chapter 30, verse 21 and shows the road leading to the cross.

HERE IS THE ROAD FOLLOW IT

Isaiah 30:21

24

GLASGOW NORTH WEST

JEREMIAH

Call to Me and I will answer You

The text is taken from chapter 33, verse 3. The Bible chapters were read and re-read until one verse stood out.

It was felt that this banner should also reflect our community and the chosen text was to lead us to our own church doorstep placed within the setting of our local countryside. Putting a decorative cross in the centre of the countryside under an archway of the text was to reflect that God's love is found everywhere. Choosing different patterned fabrics helped to formulate areas of the countryside; from fields and moorlands, to hills – including a crafty one, which was already printed with trees and bushes! Do you recognise Dumgoyne (the Sleeping Giant) and the Campsie Hills? Once the countryside background was in place, the dove, the cross and the church, which had been made by individuals, were superimposed.

25

BUCHAN WEST

LAMENTATIONS

Hope and Patience

PATIENCE

HOPE AND

Lamentations

26

HAMILTON SOUTH

EZEKIEL

The book of Ezekiel was a difficult one to understand and it was felt that no single verse would do it justice. Nine different aspects of the book were selected and illustrated. We hope the banner captures a little of the great man's vision and message for us all. Together, we had great fun creating this banner, and feel that our friendship and fellowship grew over the months it took to create.

27

WIGTOWN

DANIEL

Those who have led many to true religion shall shine like stars forever

This seemed a fitting text for a church looking back with thanksgiving for those who have brought us to knowledge of God's love in Jesus. It also calls us to look forward to a new age of mission and challenges our own witness and faith. Daniel's faith in God was a shining example, which brought others to belief. The design on the banner represents Daniel at prayer, looking towards Jerusalem. He is dressed in purple and gold; a sign of his position and high esteem.

Those who have led many to true religion shall shine like stars for ever

Daniel 12

28

STRANRAER

HOSEA

I lifted them like a little child to my cheek

This text, taken from chapter 11, verse 4, suits the Millennium theme. It reflects the essence of the all-encompassing love of God the father; holding up the child, a symbol of the dawning of a new era. This is depicted in the Millennium colours of silver and white. The artist wanted the banner to resemble a stained-glass window, modern in style, simple yet effective and distinctive.

The materials used were all donated: fabrics, sewing thread, ribbons, beads, wool, the frames and even the design itself. Loyalty, dedication, inspiration, skill and time were added!

It was not just guildmembers who took part in creating this banner. Our chosen text was the inspiration of a local minister, who passed his idea to a local artist, who planned, designed and drew up a full-scale picture, which helped to make our task easier. The husband of one of the team designed and made a simple, yet most effective, working frame. Then the banner-stand itself was made and gifted by a local hardware shop owner!

STRANRAER
PRESBYTERIAL COUNCIL

29

SOUTH ARGYLL 'A'

JOEL

I will pour out my spirit upon all people

This text reminds us of the blessings in store if we put our trust in God. The banner depicts blessings coming down on all people from the Holy Spirit.

30

SOUTH ARGYLL 'B'

AMOS

The Word of the Lord

The theme of the banner was taken from chapter 7, verses 7 and 8. A plumbline always hangs straight and true, and God promises to be true to his people. A plumbline is a simple tool but is as necessary today as it was thousands of years ago.

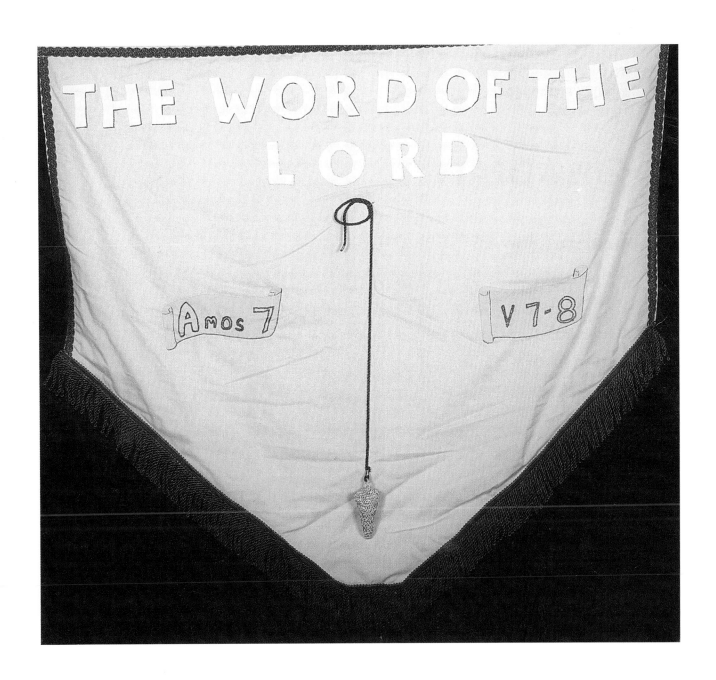

31

ENGLAND

OBADIAH

God is king

An effective illustration of this particular book in a variety of different textured fabrics.

32

LORN

JONAH

The banner illustrates the story of Jonah.

When volunteers were called for to make the Council banner, eleven guildmembers from five different Guilds came forward, each bringing a special skill, although only two of them had attended a banner-making course at Carberry. The work party met regularly in the Church Centre in Oban, over a period of eighteen months, so a considerable amount of mileage was travelled! All agreed that the task presented many challenges and problems, but the whole project provided great fun and fellowship.

LORN PRESBYTERIAL COUNCIL

Jonah disobeyed

God forgave

33

ST ANDREWS

MICAH

This banner illustrates the general theme of the Book of Micah.

34

DUNKELD & MEIGLE EAST

NAHUM

The destruction of evil in Nineveh

We had a lot of laughs in the weeks when we were making this banner, but also a lot of soul searching. It all came to a very satisfying conclusion!

Bits and pieces were donated from various places to produce this banner – including the box to transport it, begged from a local antique dealer. The bones are real – leftovers from a roast chicken!

35

ANGUS EAST

HABAKKUK

The Lord's Glory

The banner depicts the Lord's Glory, and shows one verse from each chapter.

THE LORD'S GLORY

HABAKKUK

87

36

GORDON

ZEPHANIAH

The grey background for the banner was chosen to represent the granite from which most buildings within our Presbytery are built. The sword represents God's judgement while the hands represent His grace and forgiveness. The banner depicts the main industries and activities that God's people are involved in within the Gordon area and which play such an important part in the life of this rural community: farming, fishing, hunting, castles, education, forestry, whisky, tourism, oil and the church. The text drawn from Zephaniah chapter 3, verse 15 was chosen as a prophetic word of hope offered to an economically hard-pressed rural community. The red lettering represents the great sacrifice of Christ's blood shed for us. The book, chapter and verse are highlighted by the Gordon Tartan.

The Lord, The King of Israel
has taken away your punishment,
He is with you,
never again will you fear any harm.

Zephaniah 3:15

37

BUCHAN EAST

HAGGAI

The text for this banner is taken from chapter 2, verse 9.

38

AYR

ZECHARIAH

The panel, 'The Measurement', which shows the temple in the background, not at the forefront of life in Jerusalem as it should have been, reminded us of the Church today.

The panel, 'I am coming to live among you' shows God has fulfilled His promise by sending Jesus as our Saviour. The panel, 'By My Spirit', depicts the vision of the gold lampstand representing the promise that God's people will succeed. The panel, 'The New Jerusalem' represents our hope for the future, that our Lord will return and all will be made new.

We had much fun, fellowship and hard work, making this banner. By the time we had finished we all agreed that we knew the book of Zechariah in much greater depth than we had before!

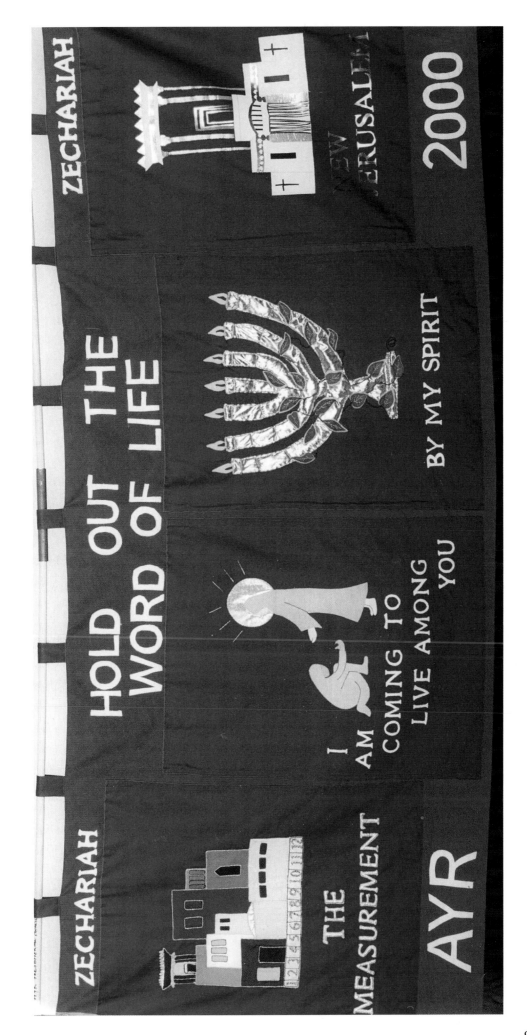

39

DUNKELD & MEIGLE WEST

MALACHI

I am the Lord I do not change: turn back to me
and I will turn back to you

*Before we started work, we had a guild meeting about making the banner.
Then our minister led a study group, and four guildmembers put pencil to
paper and attempted to pull out all the main points of God's message to
Malachi. It was felt that modern problems and transgressions should be
included. Ten members did the work, but many guildmembers added a stitch
or two. We found it gave us all a deeper understanding of Malachi and much
fellowship together.*

40

DUMBARTON

MATTHEW

The lilies of the field

The verse we chose for the banner just kept coming back to us, in spite of looking at other verses which others had suggested!

41

ABERDEEN

MARK

The banner depicts stories from Mark's Gospel:

Catching fishermen

Jesus and the children

Jairus's daughter

Feeding the five thousand

Touching the hem of Jesus' garment

The Last Supper

Forgiveness is at the heart of the Gospel.

99

42

PAISLEY

LUKE

Let God's love shine

The words of this text appealed as they were very suitable for interpretation on a banner.

43

DUNOON

JOHN

I am the true vine

This banner shows the vine and the branches.

I AM THE TRUE VINE

My Father is the husbandman.

...beareth not fruit He taketh away

Abide in me and I in you

You are the branches

The branch cannot bear fruit of itself....

I am the vine

Herein is my Father glorified,
that ye bear much fruit

St John XV (1)

44

GREENOCK

ACTS

The coming of the Holy Spirit

The banner depicts the coming of the Holy Spirit at Pentecost; the beginning of the church as we know it today.

filled with the Holy Spirit

ACTS ch2 v4

45

FALKIRK

ROMANS

The text was chosen from chapter 1, verse 8. The banner shows Christian women in the four corners of the world, all celebrating the Millennium. There are also echoes of the four seasons.

As in other Councils, this banner was made by a happy band of willing sewers, cutters and tea-makers, working together to produce this illustration of Paul's request for support.

46

STIRLING

1ST CORINTHIANS

You are God's field

The text is taken from chapter 3, verse 9 and reflects God's grace and love for us all.

All guildmembers were able to contribute, in some way, to the creation of this banner. The banner was lovingly made and a friendly joiner made the stand, and a transportation container was created out of two flower boxes. If the creation of the banner was an adventure, transporting a two-metre-long box to Edinburgh, by bus and train, to join the exhibition, was certainly another memorable day!

47

Dunfermline

2nd Corinthians

Thanks be to God for His priceless gift

The text was taken from chapter 9, verse 15. The banner is striking in its simplicity – illustrating the basis of Christian belief.

111

48

KINCARDINE & DEESIDE

GALATIANS

Service through faith

*The banner depicts guildmembers' hands reaching others through service;
that is, caring, befriending, praying, etc. It reflects the spiritual service of the
Guild in a practical form.*

49

Angus West

Ephesians

The text is taken from chapter 5, verse 9: 'for the fruit of the light consists of all goodness, righteousness and truth.'

50

MULL

PHILIPPIANS

Joy in faith

Paul's letter to the Philippians continually speaks of the joy that Christian people receive from their faith in God: the joy that Faith brings to Christian people.

51

MORAY EAST

COLOSSIANS

Taken from chapter 3, this banner illustrates that, in our daily lives, and in all we do, we need the fruits of the spirit.

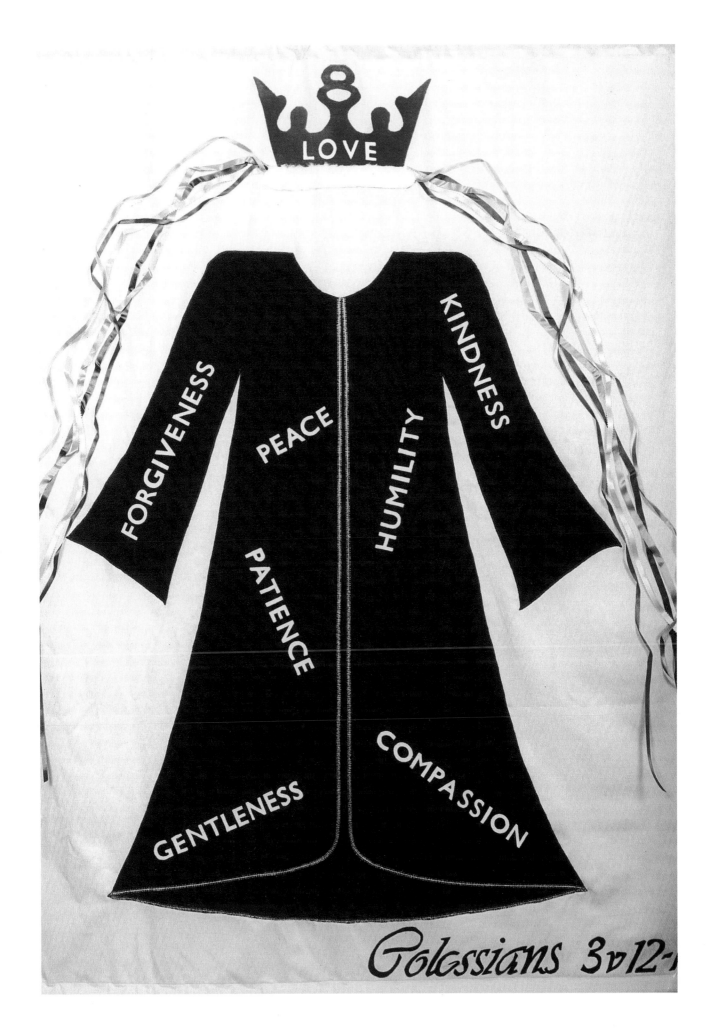

119

52

INVERNESS & NAIRN

1ST THESSALONIANS

The text is taken from chapter 5, verse 5, where Paul tells the people to walk in the light.

53

Moray West

2nd Thessalonians

Paul was telling the people to keep the Faith. This banner depicts a family looking outward to a twisting path into the sunset; into the year 2000 with Faith. It seems to embody Paul's teaching to 'go forward in Faith'.

Several Guilds commented on their initial lack of confidence and reluctance to make a banner. However, in retrospect, they realised how much community involvement, fun and hours of cheery company they had enjoyed in making them. When the exhibition was staged in Elgin, each Guild took part in the rota to welcome and steward visitors to the exhibition. All spoke of the honour and pleasure they felt when visitors from other denominations, and those who seldom entered a church, congratulated them.

54

Bute

1st Timothy

Fight the good fight

The text is taken from chapter 1, verse 18.

55

Ross – Tain

2nd Timothy

God's Word is not bound by chains

56

LOCHABER

TITUS

Sound in Faith

The text was chosen after much reading, and rereading, of the book of Titus. During our initial search for a suitable text, nothing seemed to leap out at us; you could say that our text 'sound in faith' from chapter 2, verse 2 was more dragged from the pages, and yet once we had that text we were away!

Having chosen the Sound of Arisaig as our background, the words of the text 'Sound in faith' were reflected in the shape and colours of the rainbow, reminding us of God's Promise from the beginning of time. The silhouette of the Isle of Eigg on the horizon reminds us that the letter to Titus was written to an island, and that here we have the three islands of Eigg, Muck and Rhum within our pastoral care.

In the very centre of the banner is a fishing boat with its mast representing the cross – central to our life and work. Two fishermen are in the boat representing not only the bodily food for which they toil daily, but also that they are 'fishers of men' who, through the ages, have faithfully brought people to Jesus. The fish in their variety of colours and textures represent all of Christ's people with their different gifts. The fish is also the symbol of the Christian faith. The whole village had been taking such an interest in the progress of the banner and many people were keen to see the finished article. Many conversations took place at the village Post Office in between the buying of stamps and newspapers about stitches and embroidery, and 'fish' would appear out of packets for comparison. It was an exiting day when all the pieces came together on the finished banner!

sound in faith

arisaig 1999

57

CAITHNESS

PHILEMON

God's love has set me free

After studying the book of Philemon, the group making the banner felt that it was God's love being reflected in Paul's example to Onesimus, when he was in prison, that showed the real spirit of freedom from sin.

58

KIRKCALDY

HEBREWS

Here I am, O God, to do Your Will

The text, from chapter 10, verse 9 was chosen because it reflects the fact that the letter to the Hebrews encourages the people to devote themselves to Christ. The figure on the banner represents each individual guildmember travelling along the winding road to the cross, holding up her arms to God, saying, 'Here I am, O God, to do thy will'.

When the exhibition was staged in Kirkcaldy, the museum had its busiest December for a number of years. Some 3,000 people had come through the doors! Lots of visitors came to the exhibition from many parts of the country; some visiting friends and families for Christmas. There was also a large number of non-church people!

59

LOCHCARRON & SKYE

JAMES

Show Faith by Actions

The text from chapter 2, verse 18 embodies the message of the book of James. The rays, illustrating faith in action, emanate from behind the Celtic cross.

SHOW FAITH

Love
Sincerity
Perseverance
Kindness
Honesty

Trust
Humility
Compassion
Healing
Friendship

BY
ACTIONS

JAMES CH 2

60

ABERNETHY

1ST PETER

The Word of the Lord remains forever

The text used is from chapter 1, verses 24 and 25.

After many social planning meetings, we set about getting the fabric in the colours we wanted. We thought we should have no trouble! A friend, who lived in Edinburgh, was sent to find the right shade – but to no avail! Everyone involved, whenever they went on holiday, or visited friends, scoured the shops for THE colours! Finally, a treasure-trove of a shop was found practically on our own doorstep!

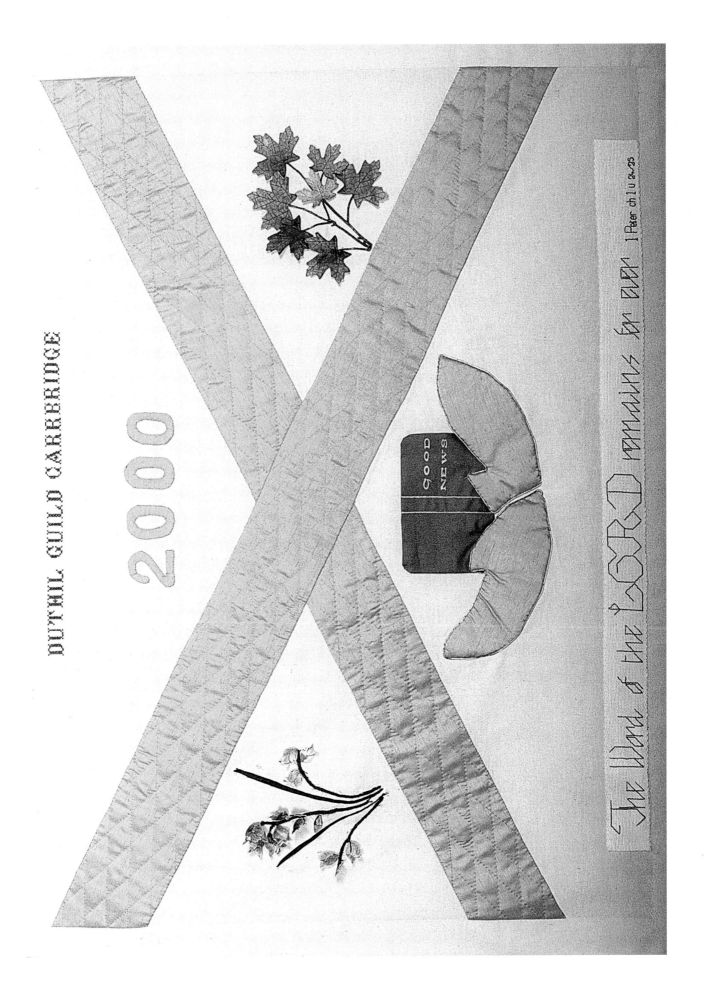

DUTHIL GUILD CARRBRIDGE

2000

GOOD NEWS

The Word of the LORD remains for ever 1 Peter ch 1 v 24-25

61

Ross

2ND PETER

The day of the Lord will come

We looked towards a new Millennium with the world encompassed within the peace of God. We felt this was reflected in the text, chapter 3, verse 10. The banner is depicted in the primary colours of earth – the bright morning star – His life, death and triumph, and the emblem of all Christians.

A banner is a means of communication; a way of conveying a message to anyone who sees it, a bold way of proclaiming a belief to the world. Our message is simple and direct. The colours represent heaven and earth, life and blood. Other symbols used show the Spirit and peace of God, the light, the community and house of God.

139

62

SUTHERLAND

1ST JOHN

God is Love

John's letter expresses love from God and we are asked to love as Jesus loves. The text chosen was taken from chapter 4, verse 16. The background of the banner is green to represent eternal life; the heart for the blood; the dove for the Spirit; the ocean for water; and the Cross reflecting faith and symbolising the Saviour of the World.

63

Lewis

2ND JOHN

This banner, on a background of Harris Tweed, shows the people of the world coming together at the cross of Christ.

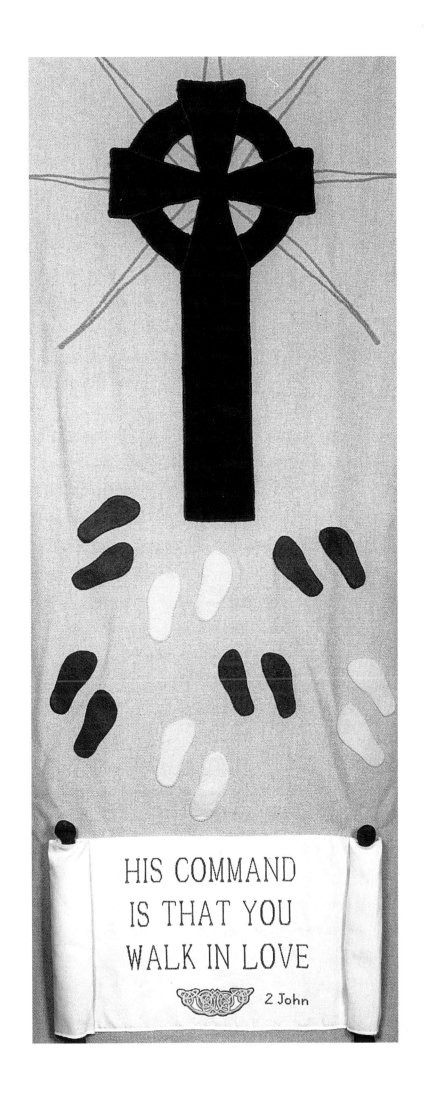

64

SHETLAND

3RD JOHN

Peace be to You

The banner shows doves of peace over the quote from the text. It seemed to represent the feelings of the 3rd Epistle of John.

65

ORKNEY

JUDE

Fight on for your Faith

We would never have chosen to seek inspiration in Jude, but, having been allocated this book, we had to! The first reading was not fruitful but, as we persevered, the strength and drama of the writing emerged. The text chosen was verses 3–13. To balance the open Bible at the foot of the picture, the text was placed prominently above the scene of storm and chaos. Jude sees this as a consequence of following false teachers who are like 'stars that have wandered from their courses'; 'trees that bear no fruit'; 'pulled up by their roots'; 'storm clouds carried away by the wind' but 'without giving rain'. Against the sun's rays, a dove symbolises Jude's greeting – 'Mercy, peace and love be yours in fullest measure'. We hope that our banner will encourage people to read this little-known book.

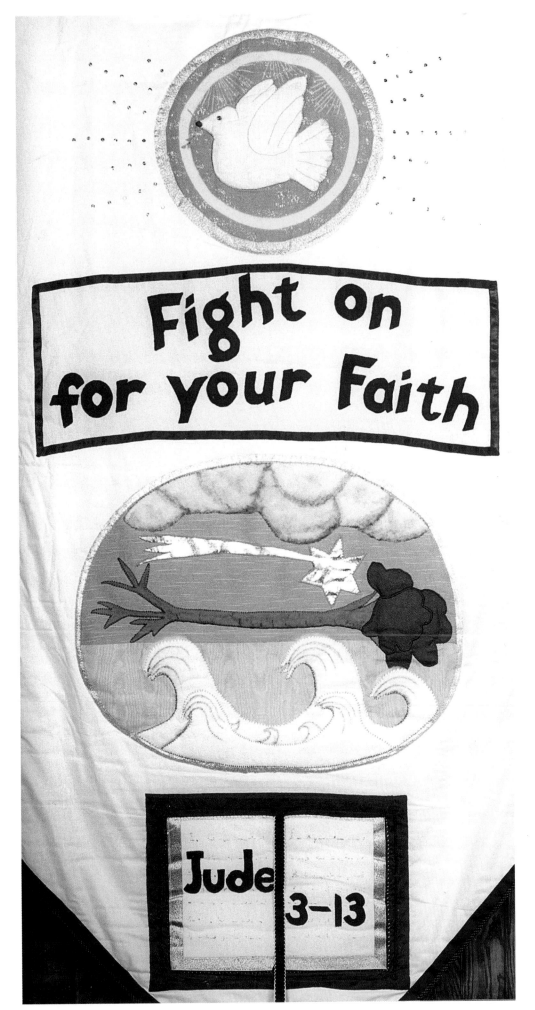

66

PERTH

REVELATION

The text was chosen from chapter 1, verse 4, as a message for the new Millennium. All the Guilds in the Council created a panel for this banner. Every Guild in the Presbytery was given a pack which included a piece of material with the Guild name drawn on it, so that it would be the correct size; the embroidery thread that had to be used; the instructions; and the date by which the embroidery had to be returned! The banner was then assembled with the cross and the dove, symbolising Grace and Peace.

67

THE NATIONAL BANNER

Taken from John, chapter 8, verse 32, 'The truth will set you free'.

The National Banner was created by eight women from across Scotland. The first step was getting to know each other and sharing our deepest beliefs. Our remit was to make a banner which would speak to people outside the church. This was a difficult task – we realised we all made so many different assumptions about belief and what people know. We kept in mind that the banner had to explain itself – people had to understand and be challenged by it!

Similarly, we were faced with the challenge of making something in step with the times – we wanted it to connect, to communicate and to witness to what we believed. One of our number woke one morning with the image of the World Wide Web, an icon of our era, and this led us to think about other webs – the web of deceit and the lies which trap us. We also wanted to communicate that we longed for everyone to know that they are loved, that to be born is to be chosen – that, we believe, is the 'truth that will set you free'.

We all experience uncertainty and ambiguity in our lives and the Good News is that God knows this and yet loves us, where we are. The challenge for each of us and the church is, as it has always been, how do we respond with compassion and without judgement, so that we may all come to know this God who sets us free – free to be the person he longs for us to be.

Thanks and acknowledgements

The Church of Scotland Guild Banners 2000 Committee would like to thank:

Guildmembers across the country who took part in banner-making for their Guild groups and Councils!

Guild Presbyterial Council Conveners and members at each of the following venues:

Wellington Church, Glasgow

St Michael's Church, Linlithgow

St Giles Church, Elgin

St Rufus Church, Keith

Old Church, Kelso

St Machar's Cathedral, Aberdeen

Old High Church, Inverness

Dornoch Cathedral, Dornoch

Kirkwall East Church, Orkney

Kilmore & Oban Church, Oban

St Columba's Church, Ayr

St Ninian's Priory, Whithorn

Glasgow Cathedral, Glasgow

St Matthew's Church, Perth

Greyfriars Church, Dumfries

St John's Church, Hamilton

St Andrew's & St George's Church, Edinburgh

St Columba's Church, London

and their ministers, Kirk Sessions and congregations; relatives, friends and helpers!

and in addition . . .

SUSAN PASFIELD AND STAFF, CAIRD HALL, DUNDEE

LAURA WOOD AND STAFF, ROYAL CONCERT HALL, GLASGOW

HARRY DUNLOP AND STAFF, ST MUNGO MUSEUM, GLASGOW

DALLAS MECHAN AND STAFF, KIRKCALDY MUSEUM, KIRKCALDY

RYDER VAN HIRE, PARTICULARLY KAYREEN AND HAMISH

CHURCH OF SCOTLAND DESIGN SERVICES DEPT, PARTICULARLY RACHEL MOWBRAY

JOHN HENDERSON, GENERAL TREASURER'S DEPT CHURCH OF SCOTLAND

PATHWAY PRODUCTIONS

KIERAN CHAMBERS, PHOTOGRAPHER

HISTORIC SCOTLAND

AND NOT FORGETTING FRIENDS AND SPOUSES OF THE BANNER COMMITTEE!

AND, IN PARTICULAR, FORMER GUILD NATIONAL PRESIDENT, MARY SHERRARD

THE COMMITTEE GRATEFULLY ACKNOWLEDGES ALL THOSE WHO HAVE DONATED MONEY
TOWARDS THIS EXHIBITION, INCLUDING A GRANT FROM THE DUNDEE CITY COUNCIL
COMMUNITY CHEST SCHEME, THUS ENSURING THAT VISITORS COULD VIEW THE
BANNERS AT NO CHARGE.

HOWEVER, WITHOUT THE GENEROUS FINANCIAL DONATION FROM THE CHURCH OF SCOTLAND,
BOARD OF NATIONAL MISSION'S AD 2000 COMMITTEE, THE HOPES AND ASPIRATIONS OF THE
COMMITTEE COULD NOT HAVE BECOME A REALITY.

. . . AND THANK YOU TO THE 25,000 PEOPLE WHO CAME . . .